I0409638

Job Strategies for the 21st Century:

How to Assist Individuals during Economic Turbulence

Dr. Daryl D. Green

WORKBOOK

This workbook corresponds with the DVD series with the same title.

"Students in today's economic fallout are feeling tremendous apprehension regarding their future in the real world. Dr. Green and Mr. Bailey provide wonderful insights in assisting students to make intelligent, informed, and strategic decisions beyond the classroom."
Brandi Reilly, Project Manager for Shaw Environmental & Infrastructure

"Dr. Green and Mr. Bailey do an excellent job of explaining how to build a life rather than just getting a job. If you are going to spend 40+ hours a week at an income-earning activity you might as well select and attain a position that fits you and for which you enjoy 'going to work' everyday. This book is a must-read for anyone who is thinking of starting a new profession or re-evaluating what he/she is currently doing."
Bruce E. Winston, PhD
Dean
Regent University
School of Global Leadership & Entrepreneurship

"Job Strategies for the 21st Century provides practical as well as inspiring insights for anyone planning on competitively advancing themself in a challenging job market. A must-read for current students and job seekers."
Ryan Zekry, New Amsterdam Bar & Grill Owner/MBA Student

Dr. Green gives the reader a clear and concise road map to conquering the job market during these turbulent times. His strategy is infused with practical ideas that should help any soon to be graduate or one-to-two year post graduate understand the job market and what it takes to market their skills for success. I wish such a book was available when I began my job search right out of college. It wouldn't have taken me years to obtain the perfect job for me!

Dr. Deshaun H. Davis,
Professor, Economist, Consultant
Northern Virginia Community College
Annandale, Virginia

"While the focus of Job Strategies for the 21st Century is to provide valuable assistance to graduating college students in formulating job strategies, it is a good read and can be an invaluable tool for individuals of all ages. It contains a little of a lot, including, statistics, advice, great quotes and good old common sense. I commend its message to anyone who is seeking success in a job market struggling to recover from our most recent recession of 2009."

Barbaralette G. Davis
Assistant City Attorney
City of Memphis

Although the authors and publisher have exhaustively researched all sources to ensure the accuracy and completeness of the information contained in this book, we assume no responsibility for errors, inaccuracies, omissions, or any inconsistency herein. Anything appearing derogatory to people or organizations is unintentional. Readers should use their own judgment or an attorney or other experts for their individual concerns.

Technical Edit by Ms. Shannon Olson

Graphic images are credited to
iStock (www.istockphoto.com) and Microsoft (www.microsoft.com).

For information on ordering in bulk, please contact:

PMLA
P.O. Box 32733
Knoxville, TN 37930-2733
(865)602-7858
advice@darylgreen.org
www.darylgreen.org

I press toward the mark for the prize of the high calling of God in Christ Jesus.

Philippians 3:14

Dedication

This workbook is dedicated to the millions of people trying to survive in these uncertain times.

Table of Contents

Preface

People are losing their jobs. Retirees are losing their retirements. US companies are losing market share due to competition abroad. Is there any wonder why college students are losing hope in finding a good job for the future? I have been to many campuses and have seen that many students are not prepared for the hectic competition for today's jobs. The original book project started as a result of my lectures during my time as a visiting professor with the National Urban League's Black Executive Exchange Program. I saw many students not prepared for the tough employment picture that was ahead for them. They just weren't ready! I was deeply moved by the students, and wanted to do more to assist all students in transitioning to full employment. In this new financial crisis, college grads must now compete with more seasoned individuals for an entry level job. Sadly, it was clear to me that many of the past approaches for college students did not consider the current economic troubles. Working with my co-author, William Bailey, our book caught the attention of many. My last book, *Job Strategies for the 21st Century: How to Assist Today's College*

Students during Economic Turbulence, has been rated number one on Amazon.com. I hope to challenge students to think about a personal job strategy for securing the right job.

Job Strategies for the 21st Century Workbook allows readers to follow my DVD series on the same subject. The workbook provides practical solutions to the challenges that today's college students face when attempting to find employment in an unstable economy. This workbook, in conjunction with the DVD series, is especially designed for frustrated parents, anxious students, bewildered professors and educators, and those who deeply care for college graduates. As adults, we must mentor our young people to discover what it is that truly makes them special. With a new sense of direction, we hope that today's college students and graduates will be encouraged to pursue their real dreams, regardless of life's circumstances.

Acknowledgement

I wish to take this opportunity first to thank God for guiding our footsteps and giving His son, Jesus, to our world. We humbly want to thank our immediate families—our wives and our children. Lord, you continue to supply us with your abundant love. You know we all need loving and supporting people to produce a special project that will be a blessing to others. Thank you for sending special people into our lives who supported us, that we, too, may be a blessing! We want to thank everyone who read, evaluated, and commented on our book. We want to especially thank my past co-author, William Bailey, for his support in this book development, and Riyam Bashir for lending her talents in my DVD series. Your critical contributions and feedback helped make this workbook a reality.

Finally, I want to thank our many friends who gave us tremendous support. There are too many to mention. I understand this accomplishment was not achieved solely on our own merit. May God continue to bless your life's journey with Him.

Introduction

Many of today's college students lack the mental toughness and fortitude

necessary to deal with economic turbulence. Today's youth must learn how

to be mentally tough if they are to survive a turbulent economic future. In

reality, many parents have crippled their children by solving their problems

for them and shielding them from making difficult decisions. This reality

can be seen in viewing 'helicopter parents' who micromanage their

children's affairs from infancy to adulthood. This has resulted in an increasing 'Boomerang Generation' of young people who move back home

and must depend on their parents for financial survival. In fact, it is a no-

brainer for college students to stay in college as long as possible so that it

can be paid for by the parents.

As the financial crisis continues, and with the US labor market severely

weakening, many college students are wondering how they will survive

these difficult times. As of March 2010, the Bureau of Labor Statistics

website reported that there were roughly 15 million people unemployed,

resulting in unemployment rate of 9.7%.[1] Simply put, landing a job today

is an extreme uphill challenge, considering the large number of graduating

students, combined with the rising number of the unemployed. With such

fierce competition today for limited jobs, understandably many wonder if

they will be able to land 'a good job' in the marketplace, while others grow

weary with the continuous stress of making ends meet.[2]

My co-author, William Bailey, and I wrote our latest book, *Job Strategies*

for the 21st Century: How to Assist Today's College Students during

Economic Turbulence. It was especially designed for frustrated parents,

---

[1] Bureau of Labor Statistics website

anxious students, bewildered professors and educators, and those who deeply care for college graduates. Through our research, we have found that there is a huge disconnect between what organizations are looking for in potential employees, and what today's graduates are providing. In this financial crisis, college grads need to be mentally tough. It is easy to see how individuals can be discouraged with the current economic recession. According to the U.S. Labor department, only 47.6% of people age 16 to 24 had jobs in August. This is the lowest percentage since the government began tracking this statistic in 1948. Yet, college grads must have the determination to overcome any crisis in life. In fact, they need to be mentally tough. Generally speaking, many young people look for the easy way out of situations. Eric Thomas, a Michigan State University administrator and motivational speaker, speaks to this revelation when talking with young people. "The problem is, you have never felt pain before. You're soft. This is a soft generation. You quit on everything." Today's college students find the employment outlook full of gloom.

---

[2] "How to overcome burnout from a dead end job," by Daryl D. Green

The Job Strategies for the 21st Century Workbook, in conjunction with the DVD series, provides today's college students and graduates with innovative strategies for positioning themselves in a tough economic market where jobs are very limited, and the economy is unstable. The workbook is designed for recent graduates, as well as nontraditional students. We recognize that today's colleges consist of more and more students who see landing a good job as a watermark in their lives.

PERSONAL NOTES:

"It is not how long you live that counts but what you do in your life that is important. You've got to learn how to deal with the storms of life."

Rev. Richard Brown, Jr.

Job Strategies for the 21st Century

For many people, the bad economic picture will not change soon enough. College students are not the exception. Economic turbulence relates to the chaos that now plagues our financial institutions, wreaking havoc on our normalcy. With a weak job growth, many U.S. jobs will continue to be outsourced globally or automated through technology. Workers now feel trapped by the current economy. In this scenario, an individual is so desperate to find 'any' job that, once they're on board, they pray that the organization will help them with their career advancement if they work hard. However, following a different strategy will assist current college students and colleges in better preparing for their future pursuits. Therefore, understanding what is happening across the world can provide more opportunities for landing the 'right' job.

The following questions pertain to the information found within this workbook and the DVD developed in conjunction with this workbook. Correct answers are provided at the end of the workbook.

Fill in the Blank:

1. _____, the development of an increasingly integrated global economy marked especially by free trade, free flow of capital, and the tapping of cheaper foreign labor markets, is upon us.

2. Companies are going toward _____ markets.

3. This is the age of the _____ worker.

4. According to the last US study, people are working an average of _____ per week, which is not enough to have or be eligible for
.

5. The issue of _____ is challenging for companies that have a social responsibility to do better.

6. According to several studies and reports, employers are saying that they cannot find _____ people to employ, and that there is a _____ shortage.

7. _____authored a book about why good people can't find jobs.

8. The job market is currently a _____market, in favor of the employers.

9. Companies are being very _____ in whom they choose to hire. They want the _____ employee.

10. Parents need to be up front with their _____of their child to graduate in _____.

11. _____is the most critical thing that employers want in an employee.

12. Parents need to allow their child to _____, and not try to solve every issue for them.

13. Professors in colleges/universities would benefit by becoming more contemporary and changing their teaching style to meet the demands of a more _____ generation.

14. Build your _____. It is how you dress, how you speak, how you distinguish yourself from others.

15. Use _____, where you fulfill the needs of a person, and they reciprocate.

16. Being employed contributes to building _____.

Please use this workbook as a planning tool to establish your plan of action and the steps involved in achieving your desired job, or one for your child. The first step to create fulfillment in your career is to evaluate what you want to do.

PERSONAL NOTES:

"And first and foremost, your education can fortify you against the uncertainties of a 21st century economy."
President Barack Obama, Hampton University Commencement 2010

CONCLUSION

During these times of rapid change and financial turmoil, college students are looking for any angle to assist them in getting the right job. In the near-term, economic turbulence will be a critical factor for most institutions. Given this outlook, some people view the future with a lot of fear. In fact, others may even feel pessimistic about their own career opportunities in the near-term. Yet, parents and students should not just give up. Hope is not lost if individuals take an active interest in their own future with proper planning.

This workbook, in conjunction with my DVD series, provides students a systematic approach to dealing with this uncertainty. Landing a 'good' job requires special character, persistence, commitment, passion, and vision to become successful. By taking control of their career strategy, college students can make a positive step in navigating these difficult economic times and landing their future jobs. Start today and achieve your desired outcome!

PERSONAL NOTES:

The ultimate measure of a man is not where he stands in moments of comfort and convenience, but where he stands at times of challenge and controversy.
- Martin Luther King, Jr., Civil Rights Leader

Answer Key

1. Globalization

2. Emerging

3. Part-time

4. 33 Hours, Benefits

5. Human Capital

6. Skilled, Skills

7. Peter Capella

8. Buyers

9. Picky/Selective, Perfect

10. Expectation, 4 Years

11. Experience

12. Mature

13. Tech Savvy

14. Brand

15. Strategic Alliances

16. Self-Esteem

About the Author

Dr. Daryl D. Green is a modern day strategist and a nationally recognized lecturer. Dr. Green loves developing intellectual properties to assist individuals with making better decisions. He is an adjunct professor at Lincoln Memorial University. He has also been a faculty member at Knoxville College. He has over 20 years of assisting organizations and individuals with making good decisions.

Currently, Dr. Green is the author of several books and writes a syndicated online column on contemporary issues, where over 3,000 online publishers/content providers around the globe have used his articles. His *FamilyVision* column, syndicated through the Newspaper Publishers Association, reached over 200 newspapers and more than 15 million readers across the country. Additionally, Dr. Green has been noted and quoted by *USA Today, Ebony Magazine,* and the *Associated Press*. He has also been a freelance writer and guest columnist for various publications, including *Knoxville News Sentinel, Knoxville Enlightener, Discovery Magazine*, and the *IEEE Technology and Society Magazine*. He has also been a special assignment reporter for the *BIG Bulletin/Reporter*.

His professional experience includes management, engineering, research and development, marketing, and personal coaching. He received a B.S. in mechanical engineering and an MA in Organizational Management. Dr. Green received a doctoral degree in strategic leadership from Regent University. He is a past talk show host, a nationally recognized lecturer, nationally syndicated columnist, and personal advisor. Before his 30th birthday, he had already managed over 400 projects, estimated at $100

million dollars. These experiences place him in a unique position for

understanding emerging trends. If you would like him to speak to your

organization or would like more information about his consulting services,

please contact:

PMLA
P.O. Box 32733
Knoxville, TN 37930-2733
Phone: (865) 602-7858
Email: advice@darylgreen.org
Home page: www.darylgreen.org

Readers' Suggestions & Input

Our company is constantly updating our products so that they are accurate and relevant. If you find missing information, want to provide some suggestions, or need additional information, please write, fax, or email us at:

PMLA
P.O. Box 32733
Knoxville, TN 37930-2733
Fax: (865) 602-7858
Email: advice@darylgreen.org

Other Books by Dr. Green

Dr. Green continues to research and produce information that aims to improve society. Below is a synopsis of some of his other products:

A Call to Destiny: How to Create Effective Ways to Assist Black Boys in America provides a practical assessment of what happens to young black boys in America. It seeks to provide ways for parents, educators, and supporters to assist these boys in their positive development. Without any intervention, young black boys, regardless of their social class, will not survive in the twenty-first century. In this book, *A Call to Destiny*, you will (a) examine the severity of the problems facing young black boys, (b) learn new strategies to bring solutions to your child and the community at large, and (c) provide inspiration to continue the fight to save this generation. (**Paperback:** 50 pages, **ISBN:** 978-1442181021)

Awakening the Talents Within is a powerful, step-by-step approach that individuals can use to solve problems and enhance their overall success. This book is a wake-up call for the next generation of leaders. Dr. Green uses his charismatic style for today's hip-hop culture, dealing with a wide range of issues from stopping procrastination to creating business ownership. The solutions contained in the book reflect over ten years of managing, consulting, and teaching in government, non-profit, business, private, and academic institutions. (**Paperback**: 136 pages, **ISBN**: 978-0595146130, **Hardcover**: 140 pages, **ISBN**: 978-0595745722)

Book Publishing for Professionals provides the secrets of gaining this useful power. Packed with proven insights and advice, this book provides simple, logical steps for professionals. It includes effective writing tools, the best publishing options, and marketing strategies to make your book successful in the marketplace. It is geared toward the writer who wants to publish a non-fiction book (biography, cookbook, self-help, Christian book, textbook, etc.). (**Paperback:** 68 pages, **ISBN:** 978-1449985561, **Kindle:** 68 pages **ASIN:** B0047T7DPA, **Hardcover:** 108 pages, **ISBN:**

978-0-557-98346-9, DVD: 26 minutes, **ASIN**: B001FB4Z3G, CD: 26 minutes, **ASIN**: B004CYFBBS)

Breaking Organizational Ties provides practical strategies for employees attempting to cope in jobs or environments which they hate. While most managers are only concerned with the bottom-line, they leave their employees vulnerable to the casualties of competitive markets. This book will enable readers to (a) learn how to survive and enjoy their time at work even in a hostile environment, (b) gain greater confidence in their ability to grow while in a downsizing organization, and (c) discover the insight to go beyond their limitations by breaking the barriers of self-doubt. (**Paperback**: 124 pages, **ISBN**: 978-1450511315)

Great Customer Service: The Definitive Handbook for Today's Successful Businesses provides a framework for businesses that want sustainable success during an unstable economy. The book appeals to sales people and anyone who wants to maintain good relationships with their customers. Readers can ensure success by following the practical application of concepts outlined in the book in order to satisfy customers' needs or wants. The book addresses the topics of building a more profitable business; increasing good sustainable customer service; inspiring workers toward great organizational performance and learning how to inspire demanding customers. (Paperback: **148 pages,** ISBN: **978-1480054707**)

Don't be an Old Fool: Common Sense & Gratitude is a collection of Dr. Green's syndicated columns through the years. The book offers practical strategies for individuals who desire to make better decisions in their lives by using sound, common-sense approaches. With renewed purpose and direction, individuals will be able to energize themselves for the future. (**Paperback**: 134 pages, **ISBN**: 978- 1466236530)

Impending Danger: The Federal Handbook for Rethinking Leadership in the 21st Century provides critical answers regarding how government leaders can reduce partisan bickering by changing the current leadership paradigm. With 40 years' worth of experience in the public sector, Dr. Green and his co-author, Dr. Gary Roberts, know what they're talking about. The book provides revelations and insights regarding political strife and the answers that can solve them. (**Hardcover:** 146 pages, **ISBN**: 978-1607971382)

More Than a Conqueror: Achieving Personal Fulfillment in Government Service is a message about how to take positive steps in achieving your goals while in government service, although any civilians will be able to benefit from this book. In *More than a Conqueror*, you will (a) go beyond your self-imposed limitations by breaking the barrier of your self-doubt and (b) protect and cultivate your life in order to bring forth the best you can in your generation. (**Paperback**: 76 pages, **ISBN**: 978-0971400887)

My Cup Runneth Over: Setting Goals for Single Parents and Working Couples guides families in setting goals for themselves. Daryl and his wife have first-hand experience on this subject, both working full-time jobs, and raising three active children. This book uses a new management process called Meshing TM. The book is very different from most family books, by focusing more on practical solutions. Dr. Green has used his and his wife's experiences as managers from government, non-profit and private business sectors to help families —regain control of their lives. Written in an informal, entertaining style, it provides information to families that gives them HOPE. Creatively illustrated with graphics and charts, the book is also indexed for quick reference. It is essential reading for families in search of purpose.
Special Awards: January Book of the Month, The Larry Young Show 1998, Special Black History Award at Atkins Library, Featured on Heaven 600 (The Top Gospel Radio Station in the Country). (**Paperback**: 108 pages, **ISBN**: 978-1889745039, **Audiobook**: 978- 1889745053, **Audio CD**: **ASIN**: B001VH787E)

Second Chance presents non-profit organizations with a way to use operations management tools for more efficiency. Non-profit organizations will become better-equipped to assist clients and constituents in meeting their needs. Dr. Green co-authored this book with one of his students. Through the eyes of student Noriko Chapman, readers will be taken on a magical journey of overcoming a difficult situation in operations management and in life. (**Paperback:** 130 pages, **ISBN:** 978-1461146070)

Selling by Objectives provides insight on how to create more sales during an economic crisis, using seven key ingredients. The book provides practical solutions that today's organizations can easily digest and implement even in an unstable economy. This book is important not only for sales people, but also for any professional involved in selling goods and services with a desire to be successful in the marketplace. Non-profit organizations, business owners, college students, professors, entrepreneurs, and other sales organizations can benefit from this book. *(**Paperback***: 138 pages, **ISBN***: 978- 1470054342)*

Writing for Professionals provides individuals with authoritative writing tools. It offers strategies, practical guidelines, resources, and a host of suggestions to help with publishing goals. The advice in this book can be useful for a wide variety of professions, including business executives, teachers, scientists, engineers, attorneys, and many others. *(**Paperback***: 240 pages, **ISBN***: 978-1475152333)*

www.ingramcontent.com/pod-product-compliance
Lightning Source LLC
Chambersburg PA
CBHW080631290526
45790CB00007B/3016